MW01639820

Reader's Digest Children's Books
Reader's Digest Road, Pleasantville, NY 10570-7000

Manufactured in China.
ISBN 1-57584-830-9
10 9 8 7 6 5 4 3 2 1

The Newborn King

The Story of the First Christmas

Retold by Allia Zobel-Nolan
Illustrated by Allan Eitzen

Pleasantville, New York • Montréal, Québec

Long ago, God asked a man named Isaiah to be his messenger. So Isaiah spoke to the people. He told them of the coming of the savior, a special baby who would save all who believe in him from their sins.

“This savior will be God’s own son,” Isaiah said. “And he will tend to his people as lovingly as a shepherd tends his lambs, feeding them and protecting them from harm.”

Many years later, a girl grew up in the town of Nazareth. Her name was Mary. When she was a young woman, she became engaged to a man called Joseph. Mary loved God very much. She prayed often, and God took notice. One day, God sent an angel to her.

"Greetings," the angel said. "The Lord is with you."

Mary looked up. She was surprised and frightened.

The angel told her not to worry. "You have found favor with God, and he has chosen you to be the mother of his son," the angel said.

At first, Mary didn't understand how this could be. But she listened as the angel explained. Then Mary bowed her head. "I will do whatever God wants," she said. When she looked up again, the angel was gone.

Then one day a message came from the king. He wanted to know how many people lived in the land he ruled. So he ordered his subjects to return to the towns where they were born to be counted.

"We must go to Bethlehem," Joseph told Mary. They left at once. Mary rode on a donkey and Joseph walked alongside her. It was a long journey, and Mary was anxious. She knew it was almost time for her baby to come.

"We will be there soon," Joseph said.

A song to sing:

"O little town of Bethlehem, how still we see thee lie!
Above thy deep and dreamless sleep the silent stars go by.
Yet in thy dark streets shineth the everlasting light;
The hopes and fears of all the years are met in thee tonight."

Something to think about:

Imagine traveling on foot or by donkey over dirt roads for three or four days in a row. That's about the time it took Mary and Joseph to travel the 70 miles (110 km) from Nazareth to Bethlehem!

At last, Joseph and Mary reached Bethlehem. They were very tired and looked forward to a good night's rest. "Do you have any rooms?" Joseph asked again and again. But he couldn't find anyplace to stay. All the inns were full.

Joseph continued to knock on doors. Finally, one kind man, seeing Mary was about to have her baby, felt sorry for them. "You can stay out back," he said, pointing to a wooden stable behind the inn. "The animals sleep there, but at least you'll have shelter for the night."

Joseph thanked the innkeeper. Then he led the way to the stable, where he and Mary slept on beds of hay.

Later that night, Mary gave birth to a baby boy. There was no tiny crib for him to sleep in; nor any soft, warm blankets to keep him warm. So Mary wrapped him in strips of cloth and laid him gently on the soft hay in the animals' feedbox.

Mary and Joseph looked down at the baby with love. The animals drew closer to see him. Somehow they knew he was special. Remembering what an angel had told him beforehand in a dream, Joseph said gently to Mary, "We will call him Jesus."

A song to sing:

"Away in a manger, no crib for a bed,
The little Lord Jesus laid down his sweet head;
The stars in the sky looked down where he lay,
The little Lord Jesus, asleep on the hay."

Something to think about:

Imagine this: Jesus, the most important baby ever born, came into the world in a stable—a shelter for cows, donkeys, and sheep.

Meanwhile, in the fields nearby, a group of shepherds were watching over their sheep. It was late, so they gathered the animals around and settled in for the night. Suddenly, a great light appeared in the dark sky. The shepherds leapt up and saw an angel of God before them. They were very frightened.

"Don't be afraid," said the angel. "God has sent me with good news. It is a happy message for everyone. Tonight, in the town of Bethlehem, a special baby is born. He is Christ the Lord. You will find him in a stable, wrapped in cloths, and lying in a feedbox."

Then the sky was filled with hundreds of angels. They were singing God's praises in loud voices, saying, "Glory to God in the highest and on earth, peace to men of goodwill."

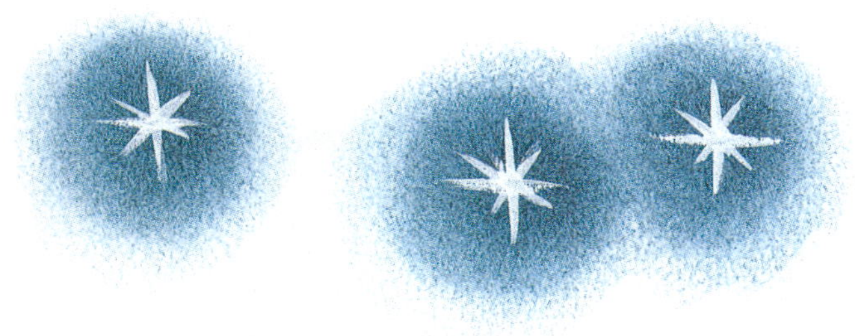

When the angels left and went back to heaven, the shepherds talked among themselves. They were amazed at what they had seen. "Let's go right away and look for the baby the angels told us about," one shepherd said. The others agreed.

The shepherds searched Bethlehem until they came upon the stable. There, they found baby Jesus as the angel had told them.

"Here is our Savior," the shepherds said.

A song to sing:

"O come let us adore him, O come let us adore him,
O come let us adore him, Christ the Lord.
For he alone is worthy, For he alone is worthy,
For he alone is worthy, Christ the Lord."

Something to think about:

Imagine how surprised the shepherds must have been—to hear news from an angel that God's son had been born.

Far off in the east, wise men noticed a new star in the sky.

"This means a great king has been born," one wise man said. "We must go find him," the others agreed. So they packed treasures of gold, frankincense, and myrrh and set off.

The wise men followed the star to a small house in Bethlehem. Inside, they found Mary and her baby. "His name is Jesus," Mary said.

The wise men knelt before Jesus and gave him their gifts. They knew at once that he was the newborn king.